THE CONSTITUTION EXPLAINED!

THE BILL OF RIGHTS

GUARANTEEING LIBERTY

BY JANEY LEVY

Gareth Stevens PUBLISHING

Please visit our website, www.garethstevens.com. For a free color catalog of all our high-quality books, call toll free 1-800-542-2595 or fax 1-877-542-2596.

Library of Congress Cataloging-in-Publication Data

Names: Levy, Janey, author.
Title: The Bill of Rights: guaranteeing liberty / Janey Levy.
Description: New York : Gareth Stevens Publishing, 2021. | Series: The constitution explained! | Includes index.
Identifiers: LCCN 2019057418 | ISBN 9781538258682 (library binding) | ISBN 9781538258668 (paperback) | ISBN 9781538258675 (6 Pack) | ISBN 9781538258699 (ebook)
Subjects: LCSH: United States. Constitution. 1st-10th Amendments–Juvenile literature.
Classification: LCC KF4750 .L485 2020 | DDC 342.7303–dc23
LC record available at https://lccn.loc.gov/2019057418

First Edition

Published in 2021 by
Gareth Stevens Publishing
111 East 14th Street, Suite 349
New York, NY 10003

Designer: Sarah Liddell
Editor: Therese Shea

Photo credits: Cover, p. 1 UbjsP/Shutterstock.com; background texture used throughout Lukasz Szwaj/Shutterstock.com; p. 5 Pgiam/E+/Getty Images; p. 7 OLIVER DOULIERY/Stringer/AFP/Getty Images; p. 9 John Lamparski/Contributor/Getty Images Entertainment/Getty Images; p. 11 A & C Wiley/Wales/Photolibrary/Getty Images Plus/Getty Images; p. 13 Mark Wilson/Staff/Getty Images News/Getty Images; p. 15 Ipsumpix/Contributor/Corbis Historical/Getty Images; p. 17 Yellow Dog Productions/The Image Bank/Getty Images; p. 19 moodboard/Brand X Pictures/Getty Images; p. 21 Fuse/Corbis/Getty Images; p. 23 Steve Mrdja/EyeEm/EyeEm/Getty Images; p. 25 RichLegg/E+/Getty Images;; p. 27 Özgür YAMAN/iStock/Getty Images Plus/Getty Images; p. 29 leezsnow/E+/Getty Images.

Printed in the United States of America

CONTENTS

WORDS IN THE GLOSSARY APPEAR IN **BOLD** TYPE THE FIRST TIME THEY ARE USED IN THE TEXT.

THE BILL OF RIGHTS: THE BASICS

You've probably heard of the Bill of Rights. But do you actually know what it is?

The Bill of Rights is a listing of individual rights and limits on the federal government contained in the first 10 amendments to the U.S. Constitution, the basic laws of the nation. Few **guarantees** of individual rights appear in the Constitution's main body.

During **debate** over approval of the Constitution, bitter arguments erupted over whether a list of individual rights was necessary. Federalists—supporters of the Constitution—argued it wasn't, since the Constitution called for a division of powers to prevent any part of the government from becoming powerful enough to threaten individual liberties. Anti-Federalists said that wasn't enough—specific individual rights would be protected only if listed. Anti-Federalists won, and the Bill of Rights was born.

CREATING THE BILL OF RIGHTS

It looked as if the Constitution wouldn't be ratified, or formally approved, without a bill of rights. So Federalists agreed to consider a series of amendments after the Constitution was approved and the new Congress met. When Congress met in 1789, Representative James Madison of Virginia created a list of 19 proposals based on suggestions from ratification debates. A committee reworked his list into 12 amendments, and the states approved 10 of them.

THE CONSTITUTION IS THE HIGHEST LAW IN THE UNITED STATES. THE AMENDMENTS THAT FOLLOW IT ARE CHANGES OR ADDITIONS TO IT.

CREATION OF THE BILL OF THE RIGHTS

1787 THE U.S. CONSTITUTION IS WRITTEN.

1788 THE CONSTITUTION IS RATIFIED.

1789 CONGRESS MEETS.
JAMES MADISON WRITES 19 AMENDMENTS.
CONGRESS CUTS THE LIST TO 12 AMENDMENTS AND SENDS THEM TO THE STATES.

1791 THE BILL OF RIGHTS IS RATIFIED AND BECOMES PART OF THE CONSTITUTION.

A CLOSER LOOK

MOST NOUNS IN THE CONSTITUTION ARE CAPITALIZED BECAUSE THAT WAS THE STYLE BACK THEN. WHEN THE BILL OF RIGHTS WAS WRITTEN, PEOPLE WEREN'T DOING THAT AS MUCH—BUT SOME WORDS WE NORMALLY WOULDN'T CAPITALIZE SNUCK IN!

THE MANY RIGHTS OF THE FIRST AMENDMENT

The First Amendment says: **"CONGRESS SHALL MAKE NO LAW RESPECTING AN ESTABLISHMENT OF RELIGION, OR PROHIBITING THE FREE EXERCISE THEREOF; OR ABRIDGING THE FREEDOM OF SPEECH, OR OF THE PRESS; OR THE RIGHT OF THE PEOPLE PEACEABLY TO ASSEMBLE, AND TO PETITION THE GOVERNMENT FOR A REDRESS OF GRIEVANCES."** What does that mean?

The U.S. Supreme Court, the nation's highest court, has ruled on cases that have to do with the Bill of Rights and helped explain what each amendment means. As for "establishment of religion," the Court has decided Congress can't pass laws that favor one religion, harm another, or get the government tangled up with religion. In interpreting the part about the free exercise of religion, the Supreme Court has said the government can't interfere with religious beliefs at all.

A CLOSER LOOK

FREEDOM OF RELIGION ISN'T PROTECTED IN PLACES SUCH AS SAUDI ARABIA, WHERE THE ONLY LEGAL RELIGION IS SUNNI ISLAM. IT ALSO ISN'T PROTECTED IN BURMA (SOMETIMES CALLED MYANMAR) WHERE MOST PEOPLE ARE **BUDDHISTS** AND FOLLOWERS OF OTHER FAITHS ARE **PERSECUTED**.

WHAT THE FOUNDING FATHERS SAID

Leaders of the young nation offer some help in understanding the religion part of the First Amendment. James Madison made it clear what it meant to him: "Congress should not establish a religion . . . nor compel men to worship God in any manner contrary to their conscience." Thomas Jefferson stated the purpose of the religion part of the amendment was to build "a wall of separation between church and state."

AMERICANS HAVE THE RIGHT TO PRACTICE THEIR RELIGION, WHATEVER IT IS—OR TO PRACTICE NO RELIGION AT ALL—WITHOUT ANY INTERFERENCE FROM THE GOVERNMENT.

Next, the First Amendment says Congress can't abridge, or limit, freedom of speech. However, a Supreme Court ruling in 1919 written by Justice Oliver Wendell Holmes Jr. said limits exist: "The most stringent [narrow] protection of free speech would not protect a man in falsely shouting fire in a theatre and causing a panic."

Congress also can't limit freedom of the press. The amendment's writers meant the government couldn't control what was printed and reported by the press. They were rejecting the British system in which only people who'd received a government license could print newspapers.

The right to peaceably, or peacefully, assemble and petition for a redress of grievances means you have a right to protest against the government and call for change. But again, limits exist. Officials may stop gatherings that threaten public safety.

A CLOSER LOOK

IN 1964, THE SUPREME COURT RECOGNIZED THE IMPORTANCE OF FREE SPEECH FOR OUR **DEMOCRACY**: "DEBATE ON PUBLIC ISSUES SHOULD BE UNINHIBITED [FREE], ROBUST, AND WIDE-OPEN, AND THAT IT MAY WELL INCLUDE VEHEMENT [FORCEFUL], CAUSTIC [HARSH], AND SOMETIMES UNPLEASANTLY SHARP ATTACKS ON GOVERNMENT AND PUBLIC OFFICIALS."

CLEAR AND PRESENT DANGER

Rights have limits. How are those limits decided? One way is the "clear and present danger" test. Supreme Court Justice Holmes wrote: "The question . . . is whether the words used are used in such a nature as to create a clear and present danger that they will bring about the substantive [substantial] evils that Congress has a right to prevent." The Supreme Court originally applied it to free speech, but it can be applied to other rights as well.

OFFICIALS CAN'T STOP A PROTEST JUST BECAUSE IT SLOWS TRAFFIC, IS ANNOYING, OR MAKES OTHER PEOPLE MAD.

THE SECOND AMENDMENT: BEARING ARMS

The Second Amendment is short, but it has caused a lot of **controversy**. Here's what it says: **"A WELL REGULATED MILITIA, BEING NECESSARY TO THE SECURITY OF A FREE STATE, THE RIGHT OF THE PEOPLE TO KEEP AND BEAR ARMS, SHALL NOT BE INFRINGED [PREVENTED]."**

Basically, this amendment is about the right to own weapons. It sounds simple, but it's turned out to be the opposite. Even today, over 200 years after the Bill of Rights was approved, people struggle to decide exactly what this amendment protects.

The problems start with the wording of the amendment itself. Experts see it as broken into two parts. How you interpret the amendment depends on which part you think should be given more importance.

A CLOSER LOOK

SOME AMERICANS HAVE CALLED FOR A **REPEAL** OF THE SECOND AMENDMENT. OTHERS HAVE ARGUED FOR BANS ON JUST CERTAIN KINDS OF DEADLY WEAPONS.

GUN OWNERSHIP IN THE UNITED STATES

According to a 2017 survey, 30 percent of American adults own a gun. Among people who live in rural areas, 46 percent own a gun. Two-thirds of gun owners say protection is the major reason they own a gun. Two-thirds of gun owners own more than one gun, with almost one-third owning five or more. Almost half of all white American men own a gun, while about one-quarter of nonwhite men own a gun.

TODAY, PEOPLE OWN GUNS TO PROTECT THEMSELVES, TO HUNT WITH, AND FOR SPORTS AND HOBBIES.

Some experts have maintained that the first part of the amendment, which ends with "state," is most important. They've argued it means the amendment's purpose is to protect states' authority to keep militias, which were groups of citizens who organized like soldiers to protect communities. Others have declared the second part is most important. It protects individuals' ownership of weapons.

In 2008, the Supreme Court stated the Second Amendment protects individual weapon ownership. The Court decided this after studying the amendment's language and comparing it to other writings of that time.

However, the Court said it was legal to place limits on who could own weapons and on where weapons could be carried. It also said laws could control weapon sales. But it didn't say exactly what limits or laws are acceptable.

A CLOSER LOOK

IN THE UNITED STATES, ABOUT 12 OUT OF EVERY 100,000 PEOPLE ARE KILLED BY GUNS EVERY YEAR. IN JAPAN, WHICH HAS TOUGH GUN CONTROL LAWS, FEWER THAN 100 OUT OF 127 MILLION PEOPLE ARE KILLED BY GUNS EACH YEAR.

MORE ABOUT LIMITS

Here's more about what the Supreme Court said regarding limits on the Second Amendment. The Court said nothing in the Second Amendment forbids laws against gun ownership by people who've been convicted of crimes and people who are mentally ill. There is also nothing against punishments for carrying weapons in schools and government buildings. In addition, the Court said a tradition exists of forbidding the carrying of "dangerous and unusual weapons."

READ BELOW TO SEE HOW THE SUPREME COURT INTERPRETED PHRASES IN THE SECOND AMENDMENT IN A CASE THEY HEARD IN 2008, *DISTRICT OF COLUMBIA V. HELLER.*

INTERPRETING SECOND AMENDMENT LANGUAGE

PHRASE	SUPREME COURT'S INTERPRETATION
KEEP AND BEAR ARMS	USE NOT LIMITED TO MILITARY ACTIVITIES
WELL REGULATED MILITIA	ALL HEALTHY INDIVIDUALS, NOT JUST ORGANIZED STATE OR FEDERAL MILITIAS

THE THIRD AMENDMENT: HOUSING OF SOLDIERS

The Third Amendment says: **"NO SOLDIER SHALL, IN TIME OF PEACE BE QUARTERED IN ANY HOUSE, WITHOUT THE CONSENT OF THE OWNER, NOR IN TIME OF WAR, BUT IN A MANNER TO BE PRESCRIBED BY LAW."**

This means the government can't force people to let soldiers live in their homes. We can't imagine the government doing this today, but practices were different when the Constitution and Bill of Rights were written.

Before the American Revolution, colonists had to provide places for British soldiers to live and supply food, firewood, and bedding for them. Colonists objected. Many saw the practice as breaking a British law that barred housing soldiers in private homes unless the owners agreed. It was because of this history that the Third Amendment was written.

A CLOSER LOOK

IN THE YEARS BEFORE THE AMERICAN REVOLUTION, BRITISH SOLDIERS WERE SUPPOSED TO BE PROTECTING THE COLONIES. HOWEVER, THE COLONISTS PREFERRED THEIR LOCAL MILITIAS FOR PROTECTION.

MORE BRITISH BACKGROUND

American colonists inherited mostly British traditions, and the British disliked standing, or permanent, armies. They objected to housing soldiers in their homes. However, they also disliked the idea of housing soldiers in buildings separate from everyone else. They feared groups of soldiers might create a military threat to people's freedoms. In the end, they concluded it was best to house soldiers in inns, stables, and private homes—but only with the owners' agreement.

CONFLICT BETWEEN BRITISH SOLDIERS AND COLONISTS LED TO A DEADLY EVENT IN BOSTON, MASSACHUSETTS, IN 1770. SOLDIERS FIRED ON A CROWD OF COLONISTS, KILLING FIVE. THE EVENT IS CALLED THE BOSTON MASSACRE.

THE FOURTH AMENDMENT: SEARCH AND SEIZURE

The Fourth Amendment says: **"THE RIGHT OF THE PEOPLE TO BE SECURE IN THEIR PERSONS, HOUSES, PAPERS, AND EFFECTS, AGAINST UNREASONABLE SEARCHES AND SEIZURES, SHALL NOT BE VIOLATED, AND NO WARRANTS SHALL ISSUE, BUT UPON PROBABLE CAUSE, SUPPORTED BY OATH OR AFFIRMATION, AND PARTICULARLY DESCRIBING THE PLACE TO BE SEARCHED, AND THE PERSONS OR THINGS TO BE SEIZED."**

This amendment has many parts, but put simply, it limits the government's power to search a person's home and seize their possessions. To conduct searches and seizures, the police must establish a good reason to convince a judge to give them a warrant, or written permission to search.

However, exceptions exist. For example, if police arrest someone for a crime, it's legal to search that person without a warrant.

A CLOSER LOOK

WARRANTS TO GATHER INFORMATION ON SUSPECTED TERRORISTS AND SPIES ARE ISSUED BY A SECRET COURT CALLED FISC (FOREIGN INTELLIGENCE SURVEILLANCE COURT). IN THE NEWS, IT'S OFTEN CALLED THE FISA (FOREIGN INTELLIGENCE SURVEILLANCE ACT) COURT.

ADDITIONAL EXCEPTIONS

Here are some more exceptions to the Fourth Amendment. If a police officer sees someone who appears to be about to commit a crime, the officer can stop that person and check for weapons. Cars can be searched without warrants in certain situations. Students' possessions may be searched at schools. Government employees' belongings may be searched at work. Prisoners may be searched in jail. Government employees may be tested for drug use without warrants too.

IF POLICE THINK YOU'VE COMMITTED A CRIME AND WANT TO SEARCH YOUR CAR FOR EVIDENCE, THEY DON'T HAVE TO GET A WARRANT FROM A JUDGE.

THE FIFTH AMENDMENT: CRIMINAL CASES

Let's look at the Fifth Amendment in two parts:
"NO PERSON SHALL BE HELD TO ANSWER FOR A CAPITAL, OR OTHERWISE INFAMOUS CRIME, UNLESS ON A PRESENTMENT OR INDICTMENT OF A GRAND JURY, EXCEPT IN CASES ARISING IN THE LAND OR NAVAL FORCES, OR IN THE MILITIA, WHEN IN ACTUAL SERVICE IN TIME OF WAR OR PUBLIC DANGER . . ."

The first section states that federal criminal charges must be started by a grand jury. A grand jury is a group of citizens who hear evidence a **prosecutor** has gathered against someone regarding criminal cases. They decide if there's enough evidence to file an indictment, or formal criminal charges.

An exception is for Americans in "land or naval" or other military forces. They're tried in military courts under different rules.

A CLOSER LOOK

THE FIFTH AMENDMENT ONLY REQUIRES A GRAND JURY IN CASES THAT WILL BE HEARD IN FEDERAL COURTS. IT DOESN'T APPLY TO CASES HEARD IN STATE COURTS, ALTHOUGH MANY STATES DO USE GRAND JURIES.

AN ANCIENT TRADITION

The history of the grand jury goes all the way back to ancient Greece. It was a well-established practice in England, and the colonists brought the practice with them to America. Its first mention in the colonies was in a writing called the Charter of Liberties and Privileges of 1683. The grand jury's basic purpose was to provide a fair means of bringing criminal charges against people who were believed to have committed crimes.

A GRAND JURY IS DIFFERENT FROM A TRIAL JURY. IT MEETS IN A SPECIAL ROOM TO DECIDE IF A CASE WILL GO TO TRIAL.

The second half of the Fifth Amendment states: "NOR SHALL ANY PERSON BE SUBJECT FOR THE SAME OFFENSE TO BE TWICE PUT IN JEOPARDY OF LIFE OR LIMB; NOR SHALL BE COMPELLED IN ANY CRIMINAL CASE TO BE A WITNESS AGAINST HIMSELF, NOR BE DEPRIVED OF LIFE, LIBERTY, OR PROPERTY, WITHOUT DUE PROCESS OF LAW; NOR SHALL PRIVATE PROPERTY BE TAKEN FOR PUBLIC USE, WITHOUT JUST COMPENSATION [PAYMENT]."

This part protects a person from being tried twice for the same crime. This is commonly called the "double jeopardy clause." Exceptions exist, such as when a jury can't decide.

The amendment guarantees that someone accused of a crime won't have to provide **incriminating** evidence. It also promises everyone due process of law, a phrase that means fair treatment in the legal system.

EMINENT DOMAIN

The last part of the Fifth Amendment has nothing to do with criminal cases. It's about the government's right to take private property for public use, such as a road. This power is called eminent domain. The amendment says the government must pay the property owner a fair amount for the property. Who decides what's a fair amount? The amendment doesn't say. It may be a jury, a judge, or a special decision-making group.

SOMETIMES A WITNESS IN A TRIAL "TAKES THE FIFTH." THAT MEANS THEY'RE REFUSING TO ANSWER A QUESTION BASED ON THEIR FIFTH AMENDMENT RIGHT NOT TO PROVIDE EVIDENCE THAT WOULD MAKE THEM SEEM GUILTY OF A CRIME.

A CLOSER LOOK

BECAUSE OF THE FIFTH AMENDMENT, THE SUPREME COURT RULED THAT POLICE MUST TELL ANYONE THEY ARREST THAT THEY HAVE THE RIGHT TO REMAIN SILENT, THAT ANYTHING THEY SAY MAY BE USED AGAINST THEM IN COURT, AND THAT THEY HAVE THE RIGHT TO A LAWYER.

THE SIXTH AMENDMENT: A FAIR TRIAL

The Sixth Amendment begins: **"IN ALL CRIMINAL PROSECUTIONS, THE ACCUSED SHALL ENJOY THE RIGHT TO A SPEEDY AND PUBLIC TRIAL, BY AN IMPARTIAL JURY OF THE STATE AND DISTRICT WHEREIN THE CRIME SHALL HAVE BEEN COMMITTED, WHICH DISTRICT SHALL HAVE BEEN PREVIOUSLY ASCERTAINED [IDENTIFIED] BY LAW . . ."**

This amendment is about making sure someone accused of a crime receives a fair trial. They have a right to a speedy trial after they've been charged with a crime. "Speedy" means a reasonable amount of time rather than quick.

Next, the amendment says the accused gets a public trial with a jury. This helps assure fairness and is considered a way to protect people from government persecution. The jury must be impartial. It must be representative of the community and not be **biased**.

A CLOSER LOOK

THE RIGHT TO A SPEEDY TRIAL GOES ALL THE WAY BACK TO A BRITISH **DOCUMENT** FROM 1215 CALLED THE MAGNA CARTA.

A DIFFERENT TIME

When the Bill of Rights was written, no professional police existed. Ordinary men took turns acting as police. Victims, not prosecutors, usually began criminal cases. There were often no lawyers at trials, just victims and **defendants** who argued their own cases. Juries, made up of 12 men, knew the victim, defendant, and witnesses. Juries considered both whether the defendant was guilty and whether they deserved mercy if they were guilty.

THE TIME BEFORE AN ARREST, WHEN POLICE ARE GATHERING EVIDENCE AND INTERVIEWING WITNESSES TO A CRIME, ISN'T CONSIDERED WHEN DETERMINING WHETHER OR NOT A TRIAL HAS BEEN SPEEDY. THAT PERIOD MAY TAKE YEARS.

The second part of the Sixth Amendment says that the accused has the right **"TO BE INFORMED OF THE NATURE AND CAUSE OF THE ACCUSATION; TO BE CONFRONTED WITH THE WITNESSES AGAINST HIM; TO HAVE COMPULSORY PROCESS FOR OBTAINING WITNESSES IN HIS FAVOR, AND TO HAVE THE ASSISTANCE OF COUNSEL FOR HIS DEFENSE."**

This means the accused has the right to know exactly what crime they're accused of. Each witness against the accused must appear at the trial so they can be questioned and the jury can decide if they can be believed. The accused has the right to call witnesses and present their own interpretation of the facts. And, importantly, the accused is entitled to a lawyer. If they can't afford one, one will be appointed for them.

THE RIGHT TO A LAWYER

When the Sixth Amendment was written, the idea that the accused could have a lawyer seemed to apply only to people who could afford one. It wasn't until 1938 that the Supreme Court ruled that anyone who couldn't afford a lawyer would have one chosen for them. The Court said the right to have the help of a lawyer "is necessary to insure fundamental human rights of life and liberty."

THE SIXTH AMENDMENT ALSO REQUIRES THAT FEDERAL CRIMINAL CASES BE TRIED IN THE STATE AND DISTRICT IN WHICH THE CRIME WAS COMMITTED. YOU CAN'T BE TRIED IN OKLAHOMA FOR A CRIME YOU COMMITTED IN NEW YORK.

A CLOSER LOOK

NOT ALL COUNTRIES OFFER THE RIGHTS CONTAINED IN THE SIXTH AMENDMENT. IN CHINA, FOR EXAMPLE, POLICE CAN SECRETLY HOLD PEOPLE FOR UP TO SIX MONTHS. THESE PEOPLE CAN'T CONTACT THEIR LAWYER, THEIR FAMILY, OR ANYONE ELSE.

THE SEVENTH AND EIGHTH AMENDMENTS

The Seventh Amendment says: **"IN SUITS AT COMMON LAW, WHERE THE VALUE IN CONTROVERSY SHALL EXCEED TWENTY DOLLARS, THE RIGHT OF TRIAL BY JURY SHALL BE PRESERVED, AND NO FACT TRIED BY A JURY, SHALL BE OTHERWISE REEXAMINED IN ANY COURT OF THE UNITED STATES, THAN ACCORDING TO THE RULES OF THE COMMON LAW."** This means the right to trial by jury exists for noncriminal cases, called civil cases, in federal courts. Also, juries' decisions usually can't be reexamined or retried by another court.

The Eighth Amendment says: **"EXCESSIVE BAIL SHALL NOT BE REQUIRED, NOR EXCESSIVE FINES IMPOSED, NOR CRUEL AND UNUSUAL PUNISHMENTS INFLICTED."** This stops the federal government from making penalties that are too harsh. The part about cruel and unusual punishments was added because people feared the federal government might use punishment unfairly.

A CLOSER LOOK

IN THE SEVENTH AMENDMENT, THE ARGUMENT IN A CIVIL CASE MUST INVOLVE AT LEAST $20 TO BE HEARD IN A FEDERAL COURT. THAT WAS A LOT OF MONEY THEN. TODAY, THE AMOUNT IS AT LEAST $75,000.

WHAT IS CRUEL AND UNUSUAL?

There's a lot of debate about the "cruel and unusual punishment" part of the Eighth Amendment. Is only awful punishment forbidden, or does it forbid punishment that doesn't match the crime? Is the death penalty cruel and unusual for a terrible crime? What about locking someone up alone for a long time? The Supreme Court has said that torture is cruel and unusual. Taking away someone's citizenship is also cruel and unusual.

CIVIL CASES ARE ABOUT DISPUTES BETWEEN TWO OR MORE PARTIES. SUPPOSE YOU SLIPPED ON A WET FLOOR IN A STORE AND HURT YOURSELF. IF THE STORE DIDN'T PUT UP A WET-FLOOR SIGN, YOU COULD START A CIVIL CASE TO GET MONEY FOR YOUR INJURIES.

THE NINTH AND TENTH AMENDMENTS

The Ninth Amendment says: **"THE ENUMERATION IN THE CONSTITUTION, OF CERTAIN RIGHTS, SHALL NOT BE CONSTRUED TO DENY OR DISPARAGE OTHERS RETAINED BY THE PEOPLE."** This means the rights enumerated, or listed, in the Bill of Rights aren't all the rights Americans have.

The Tenth Amendment says: **"THE POWERS NOT DELEGATED TO THE UNITED STATES BY THE CONSTITUTION, NOR PROHIBITED BY IT TO THE STATES, ARE RESERVED TO THE STATES RESPECTIVELY, OR TO THE PEOPLE."** This means the federal government only gets those powers specifically given to it by the Constitution. The states and the people have all other powers.

What do all these amendments have in common? They mean that YOU, as an American citizen, have rights and power. Be proud to exercise your constitutional rights!

A CLOSER LOOK

SEVENTEEN OTHER AMENDMENTS WERE ADDED TO THE CONSTITUTION AFTER THE BILL OF RIGHTS. THERE ARE 27 IN ALL.

WAS ADDING THE BILL OF RIGHTS DANGEROUS?

During debate over the Constitution, some argued that adding the Bill of Rights was dangerous. The act of listing rights of the people might suggest the federal government had powers it hadn't been given. And since any list of rights would be incomplete, it might suggest people didn't have those rights not listed. It was to address these concerns that the Ninth and Tenth Amendments were created.

SOME PEOPLE SAY THE BILL OF RIGHTS IS A LIVING DOCUMENT. THEY BELIEVE OUR INTERPRETATION OF IT SHOULD CHANGE AS SOCIETY CHANGES. OTHERS THINK IT SHOULD BE INTERPRETED ONLY AS THOSE WHO WROTE IT WOULD HAVE INTERPRETED IT. WHAT DO YOU THINK?

Bill of Rights

Congress OF THE United States,

begun and held at the City of New York, on Wednesday, the fourth of March, one thousand seven hundred and eighty nine.

The Conventions of a number of the States having, at the time of their adopting the Constitution, expressed a desire, in order to revent misconstruction or abuse of its powers, that further declaratory and restrictive clauses should be added: And as extending the ground of public confidence in he Government, will best insure the beneficent ends of its institution:

Resolved, by the SENATE and HOUSE of REPRESENTATIVES of the UNITED STATES of AMERICA in Congress assembled, wo thirds of both Houses concurring. That the following Articles be proposed to the Legislatures of the several States, as Amendments to the Constitution of the United tates; all, or any of which articles, when ratified by three fourths of the said Legislatures, to be valid to all intents and purposes, as part of the said Constitution, viz.

Articles in addition to, and Amendment of the Constitution of the United States of America, proposed by Congress, and ratified y the Legislatures of the several States, pursuant to the fifth Article of the Original Constitution.

rticle the first ...... After the first enumeration required by the first Article of the Constitution, there shall be one Representative for every thirty thousand, until the number shall amount to one hundred, after which, the proportion shall be so regulated by Congress, that there shall be not less than one hundred Representatives, nor less than one Representative for every forty thousand persons, until the number of Representatives shall amount t hundred, after which, the proportion shall be so regulated by Congress, that there shall not be less than two hundred Representatives, n than one Representative for every fifty thousand persons. [Not Ratified]

rticle the second .... No law, varying the compensation for the services of the Senators and Representatives, shall take effect, until an election of Represen shall have intervened. [Not Ratified]

rticle the third ...... Congress shall make no law respecting an establishment of religion, or prohibiting the free exercise thereof; or abridging the freedom of speech,

GLOSSARY

bail: an amount of money given to a court to allow a prisoner to leave jail, with the promise to return later for a trial

bias: to have an unfair preference or dislike of something

Buddhist: someone who follows a popular religion of eastern and Central Asia that focuses on the teachings of Gautama Buddha

controversy: strong disagreement about something among a large group of people

debate: an argument or public discussion

defendant: a person accused of a crime in a court of law

democracy: a government in which every person has the free and equal right to participate

document: a formal piece of writing

guarantee: a written promise. Also, to promise.

incriminating: causing someone to appear guilty of something

persecute: to make a group of people suffer cruel or unfair treatment

prosecutor: the lawyer in a court case who tries to prove that the accused person is guilty

repeal: to do away with a law

terrorist: one who uses violence and fear to challenge an authority

FOR MORE INFORMATION

BOOKS

Bjorklund, Ruth. *The Bill of Rights: Why It Matters to You.* New York, NY: Children's Press, 2019.

Kawa, Katie. *Bill of Rights.* New York, NY: PowerKids Press, 2017.

Leavitt, Amie Jane. *The Bill of Rights in Translation: What It Really Means.* North Mankato, MN: Capstone Press, 2018.

WEBSITES

The Bill of Rights
www.history.com/topics/united-states-constitution/bill-of-rights
Learn more about what and who shaped the Bill of Rights.

The Bill of Rights: A Transcription
www.archives.gov/founding-docs/bill-of-rights-transcript
Read the full text of the 12 amendments sent to the states, as well as the 10 amendments that became the Bill of Rights.

What Does It Say?
www.archives.gov/founding-docs/bill-of-rights/what-does-it-say
Read the Bill of Rights rewritten in modern English here.

INDEX